HOW TO DRAW FANTASY ART

MAGICAL KINGS AND QUEENS

Steve Beaumont

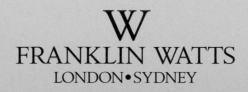

FRANKLIN WATTS
LONDON • SYDNEY

First published in 2007 by Franklin Watts

Copyright © 2007 Arcturus Publishing Limited

Franklin Watts
338 Euston Road
London NW1 3BH

Franklin Watts Australia
Level 17/207 Kent St, Sydney, NSW 2000

Produced by Arcturus Publishing Limited,
26/27 Bickels Yard, 151–153 Bermondsey Street, London SE1 3HA

Artwork and text: Steve Beaumont
Editor: Alex Woolf
Designer: Jane Hawkins

A CIP catalogue record for this book is available from the British Library.

Dewey Decimal Classification Number: 743'.87

ISBN: 978 0 7496 7652 0

Printed in China

Franklin Watts is a division of Hachette Children's Books.

Contents

Introduction

If you've picked up this book, you are probably a big fan of sword-and-sorcery movies, books or games. You may be one of those fans who enjoys the genre so much that you'd like to have a go at creating some magical characters for yourself. If so, this book will help you get started on the right path.

One of the best things about drawing fairytale kings and queens and other fantasy figures is that – apart from the basic rules of anatomy and perspective – there are no other rules. In fantasy art, no one can tell you that a character's nose is too long or her crown is the wrong shape – these are products of your imagination and you can draw them exactly as you please!

Kings

Ruler of his land, ruler of his people: the weight of such responsibility could only be carried on the shoulders of a great man. In the days when kingdoms regularly waged war on each other, a king's people needed to feel safe and secure in the knowledge that their ruler was brave of heart and fierce of sword: a big man with a big heart. Unfortunately, power can sometimes corrupt a man's heart and mind, creating evil kings, who oppress their people and rule only for themselves.

Queens

In sword and sorcery, the responsibility of leadership does not always fall on the shoulders of male characters. Many kingdoms are ruled, and many a battle has been won, by a strong-minded woman with an iron will. As with kings, there are both good and evil queens, and in this book you will encounter both extremes.

Equipment

To start with, you'll need the tools of the trade. Decent materials and equipment are essential if you want to produce high-quality illustrations.

Paper

For your practice sketches, buy some cheap A4 or A3 paper from a stationery shop. When practising ink drawing, use line art paper, which can be purchased from an art or craft shop.

For painting with watercolours, use watercolour paper. Most art shops stock a large range of weights and sizes – 250 g/m or 300 g/m is fine.

Pencils

Get a good range of lead pencils ranging from soft (6B) to hard (2H). Hard-leaded pencils last longer and leave fewer smudges on your paper. Soft-leaded ones leave darker marks on the paper and wear down more quickly. 2H pencils are a good medium-range product to start with.

For fine, detailed work, mechanical pencils are ideal. These are available in a range of lead thicknesses, 0.5 mm being a good middle range.

Pens

For inking, use either a ballpoint or a simple dip pen and nib. For colouring, experiment with the wide variety of felt-tips on the market.

Markers

These are very versatile pens that, with practice, can give very pleasing results.

Brushes

Some artists like to use a fine brush for inking line work. This takes a bit more practice to master, but the results can be very satisfying. If you want to try your hand at brushwork, you will need some good-quality sable brushes.

Watercolours and gouache

Most art shops will also stock a wide range of these products from student to professional quality.

Inks

Any good brand will do.

INDIAN INK

Eraser

There are three types of eraser: rubber, plastic and putty. Try all three to see which you prefer.

Oh, and you may need something for sharpening your pencils...

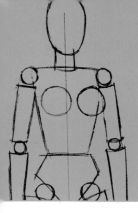

Basic Construction

Before we start on some projects, let's look at an easy way of constructing human figures. In fantasy illustration, all characters can be broken down into geometric shapes.

Anyone who can hold a pencil can draw two-dimensional geometric shapes such as squares, triangles and circles. But this on its own will not make your characters seem real. If you can draw three-dimensional shapes such as cylinders, cubes, spheres and egg shapes, it will help to give form and solidity to your characters. Here are some examples.

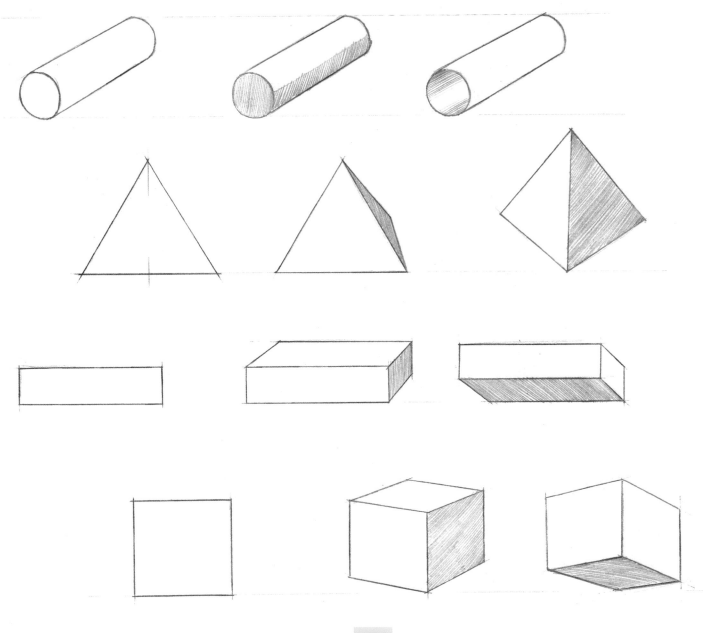

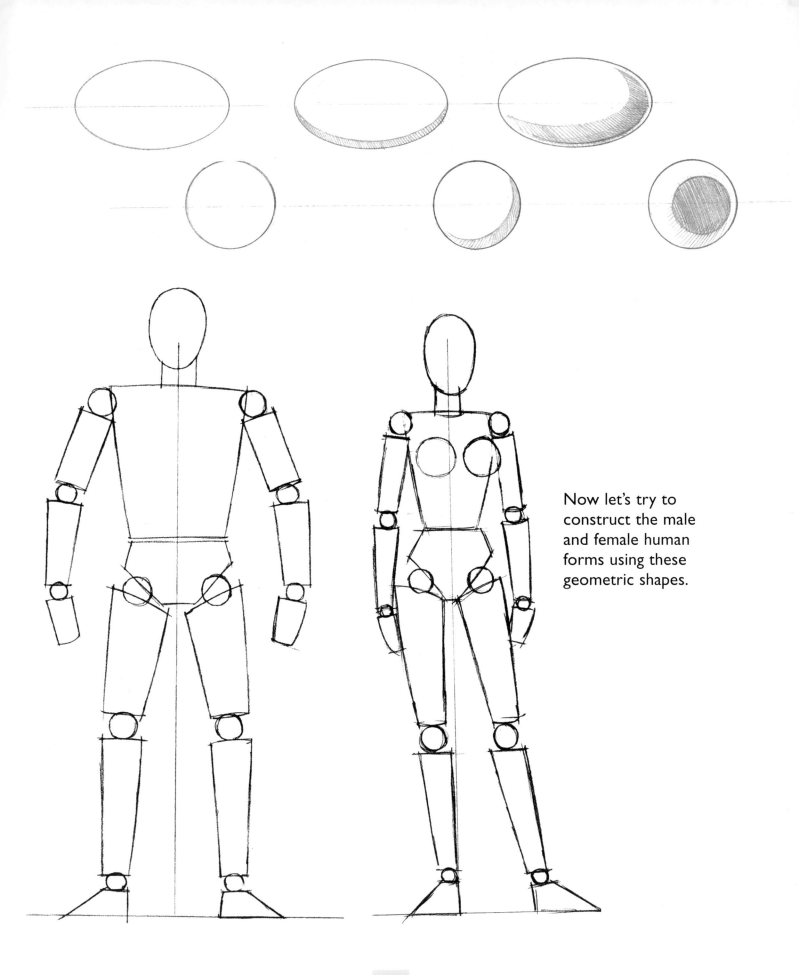

Now let's try to construct the male and female human forms using these geometric shapes.

Good King

The pose we have chosen for this king suggests that, although he is mighty, he uses his power wisely. Respected by his subjects and feared by his enemies, he is the type of king who thinks before he acts. But if he is attacked, he will not hesitate to raise his heavy sword.

Stage 1
Start with a stick figure to establish the basic shape. Construct a solid, regal pose.

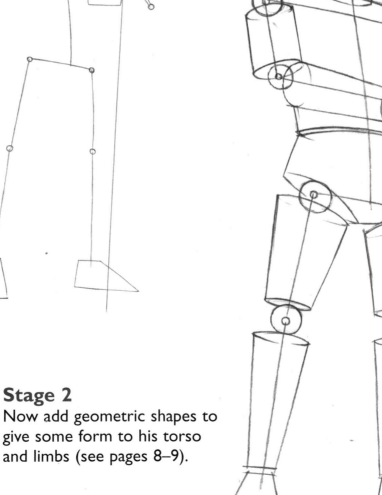

Stage 2
Now add geometric shapes to give some form to his torso and limbs (see pages 8–9).

Stage 3

Now add the outer body form and the facial features. Try practising different facial expressions before applying one to your drawing. The king's face should show his strength of character. Add a bushy beard to complete it.

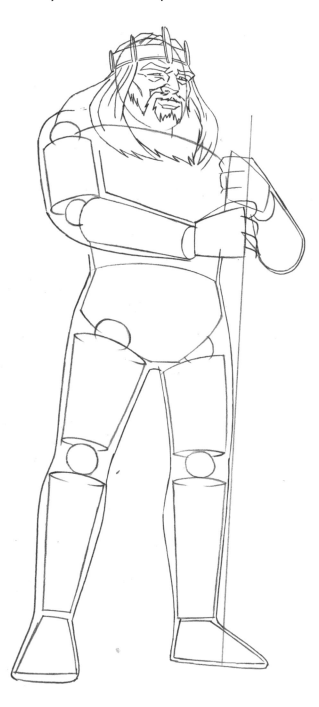

Stage 4

This is not the type of king to dress in rich, fancy clothing. His garments will be of the finest material but they will also be functional enough for battle. Give him heavy-duty leather breastplates, gloves, boots and a hefty broadsword. Place a cloak around his shoulders.

Stage 5
Refine the detail in his hair and armour and add some shading to give definition to his overall form.

Stage 6
Start to apply ink to the figure.

Stage 7
Note how the use of solid areas of black ink gives strength to this drawing.

Stage 8

You can colour your drawing, if
you like, using marker pens, felt-
tips or watercolours. Lay down
each colour in one continuous
wash if you can, applying the
colour as smoothly as possible.
The colours that suit this king
are rich, warm browns and reds.

Evil King

This king, who probably obtained his crown by foul means, craves only power and riches. He is devious, spiteful and forever suspicious of plots against him. No brave heart here — just a black one, twisted and cruel.

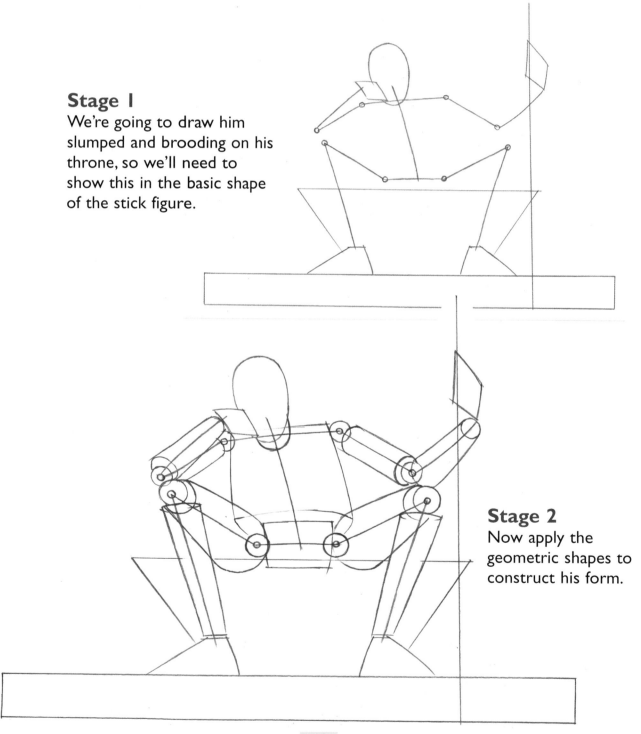

Stage 1
We're going to draw him slumped and brooding on his throne, so we'll need to show this in the basic shape of the stick figure.

Stage 2
Now apply the geometric shapes to construct his form.

Stage 3
Smooth out the body form and draw in his scowling face. Add hair and a crown.

Stage 4
Erase the geometric shapes and give him clothes, including boots, gloves and a belt. Start shaping his throne.

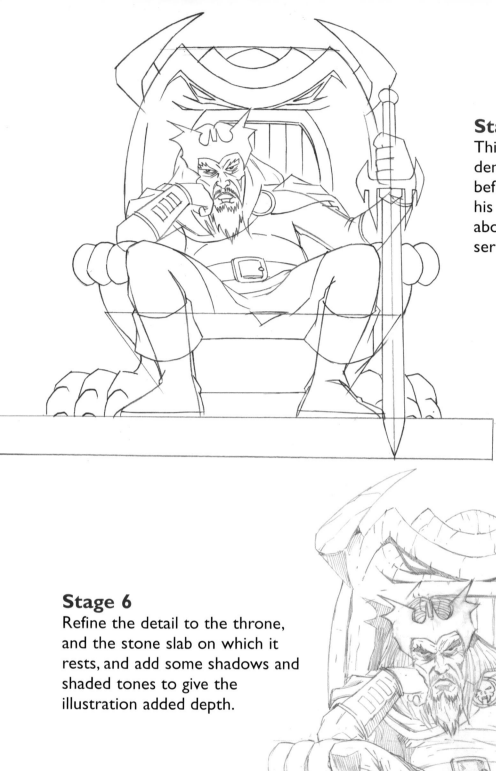

Stage 5
This throne resembles a devil or demon – the kind of throne that befits an evil king. Place a sword in his hand, making him look as if he is about to use it on an annoying servant.

Stage 6
Refine the detail to the throne, and the stone slab on which it rests, and add some shadows and shaded tones to give the illustration added depth.

Stage 7
Start to ink in the drawing.

Stage 8
Note that the use of solids helps to create the mood and tone of this image.

Stage 9

Since this character is consumed by evil, it may seem a good idea to seat him on a black throne. Although this would look cool, it wouldn't help to display the king very well. So, to add some contrast, we'll show the throne as a heavy timber construction.

Good Queen

Although this queen seems a young woman, she has a wise head on her shoulders, and rules with kindness and fairness. A fantasy character's looks don't always tell the whole story — often those who appear mere youngsters are actually old beyond their years.

Stage 1
We're going to give this character poise and elegance, so we'll draw the stick figure as though it is standing still rather than in motion.

Stage 2
Apply the geometric shapes, remembering to keep the body tall and slender.

Stage 3

Add the facial features and a suitable crown. Note that female faces are thinner and more refined than male faces, with larger eyes and fuller lips.

Stage 4

Give her clothing and a sword. It's always useful to study history books that contain pictures of medieval rulers to get ideas for costumes. You don't have to copy them exactly, but it gives you a good starting point for creating your own outfits.

Stage 5

Add further details to the costume, such as delicate embroidery on the bodice and folds in the gown. Note that the decoration on this sword distinguishes it from an everyday battle weapon.

Stage 6

Now start applying the ink, keeping the lines fine and delicate.

Stage 7
The solid shadow of her high collar has helped to define her face. However, the overall look is still light.

Stage 8

Finally, apply colour, if you wish to. Using bright, warm yellows and golds helps to establish this character as a force for good.

Evil Queen

This queen's looks also reflect her personality. She's clearly a ruthless woman who will stop at nothing in her quest for power over everybody and everything. She is prepared to use every trick in the book to get what she desires.

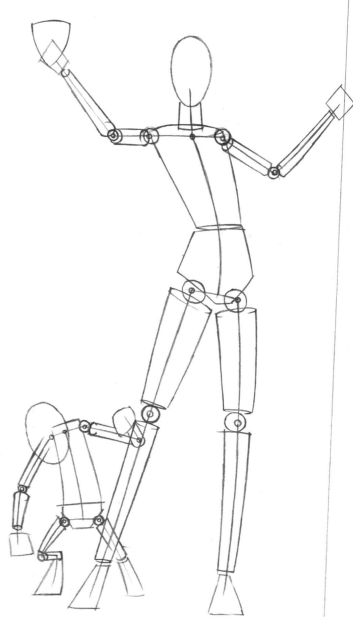

Stage 1
We want to show our queen as an imposing figure who strikes fear in the hearts of her subjects. So we'll use a more dynamic pose for the stick figure than we did for the good queen. To add to the effect, we'll include a little demonic sidekick at her feet.

Stage 2
Use long cylinders for the queen's limbs when adding the geometric shapes, and short ones to create a stunted frame for her little helper.

Stage 3

Although the facial features are attractive, they also have a certain haughtiness, to convey cruelty. Have as much fun as you like creating an ugly face for her pet. At this stage we can add the outer body form.

Stage 4

Now erase the geometric shapes and add in the outline of her costume. Note how it gives her the appearance of a demon or some creature of the night.

Stage 5
The horned headdress reinforces the aura of evil that surrounds this queen. Place a steaming goblet of evil potion in one hand and a mystical staff, complete with magic crystal, in the other.

Stage 6
Now finish off the pencil sketch by adding a few final details and some shading. At this stage we decide that most of her costume will be solid black in the final drawing.

Stage 7

Now begin to apply the ink. Create shading by drawing closely spaced parallel lines, known as crosshatching.

Stage 8

Note that the inking is heavier here than on previous drawings. There are large areas of solid black, leaving very little detail in the costume or the drawing as a whole. This simple use of solid black adds greatly to the impact of the image.

Stage 9

The use of purple clearly defines this queen as evil. Note the pale tone of her skin – the poor girl is probably allergic to daylight! Green is always a good choice for pesky-looking demons.

Glossary

anatomy The physical structure of a human or other organism.

aura A distinctive impression created by somebody or something.

bodice The part of a woman's dress that covers the upper body.

broadsword A sword with a wide, flat blade, designed for cutting rather than thrusting.

contrast An effect created by placing different colours or shades next to each other.

corrupt Make someone or something become immoral or dishonest.

crosshatching Parallel or intersecting lines drawn across part of a drawing, usually diagonally, to give the effect of shadow.

cylinder A shape with straight sides and circular ends of equal size.

demonic Like a demon.

dynamic Full of energy.

embroidery The use of needlework to make decorative designs.

facial *adjective* Of the face.

functional Having a practical purpose.

geometric shape Simple shapes, such as cubes, spheres and cylinders.

gouache A mixture of non-transparent watercolour paint and gum.

haughtiness Arrogance.

imposing Creating an impression of importance and grandeur.

mechanical pencil A pencil with replaceable lead that may be advanced as needed.

medieval Relating to the Middle Ages in Europe (approximately 1000 to 1500 AD).

mystical Something with supernatural or spiritual significance or power.

oppress To subject a people to harsh rule.

perspective In drawing, changing the relative size and appearance of objects to allow for the effects of distance.

poise Calm and self-assured dignity.

potion A drink with magical powers.

refined Graceful and elegant.

regal Royal.

sable brush An artist's brush made with the hairs of a sable, a small mammal from northern Asia.

sphere An object shaped like a ball.

stick figure A simple drawing of a person with single lines for the torso, arms and legs.

stunted Something of restricted growth.

tone Any of the possible shades of a particular colour.

torso The upper part of the human body, not including the head and arms.

watercolour Paint made by mixing pigments (substances that give something its colour) with water.

Further Information

Books

Drawing and Painting Fantasy Figures: From the Imagination to the Page by Finlay Cowan (David and Charles, 2004)

Draw Medieval Fantasies by Damon J. Reinagle (Peel Productions, 1995)

How to Draw Fantasy Characters by Christopher Hart (Watson-Guptill Publications, 1999)

How to Draw Wizards, Dragons and other Magical Creatures by Barbara Soloff Levy (Dover Publications, 2004)

Kids Draw Knights, Kings, Queens and Dragons by Christopher Hart (Watson-Guptill Publications, 2001)

Websites

drawsketch.about.com/od/drawfantasyandscifi/tp/imagination.htm
Advice on drawing from the imagination.

elfwood.lysator.liu.se/farp/art.html
An online guide to creating your own fantasy art.

Note to parents and teachers:

Every effort has been made by the publishers to ensure that these websites are suitable for children and contain no inappropriate or offensive material. However, because of the nature of the Internet, it is impossible to guarantee that the contents of these sites will not be altered. We strongly advise that Internet access is supervised by a responsible adult.

Index